the breath you take from the lord

the breath you take from the lord

Patrick Friesen

HARBOUR PUBLISHING

Harbour Publishing
P.O. Box 219
Madeira Park, BC
Canada V0N 2H0

Website: www.harbourpublishing.com

THE CANADA COUNCIL | LE CONSEIL DES ARTS
FOR THE ARTS | DU CANADA
SINCE 1957 | DEPUIS 1957

We acknowledge the financial support of the Government of Canada through the Book Publishing Industry Development Program for our publishing activities. We further acknowledge the support of the Canada Council for the Arts and the Province of British Columbia through the British Columbia Arts Council for our publishing program.

Printed in Canada
Cover design and author photograph by Marijke Friesen
Cover photographs by Margaret Friesen

National Library of Canada Cataloguing in Publication Data

Friesen, Patrick, 1946–
    the breath you take from the lord

Poems.
ISBN 1-55017-284-0

I. Title.
PS8561.R496B73 2002   C811'.54   C2002-910767-9
PR9199.3.F77B73 2002

Contents

träumerei (1997-2000)

clearing poems

1

late afternoon sun blazes off birch trees and you're caught by a
    clearing where you were born
you know that light like you know breath like you know the
    unnamed earth around you
you remember how the mind moved rustling like a small animal in
    underbrush skittering among the leaves

there is room for sadness here this is the place where a boy
    understands more than he knows
barbed wire and wild roses the tangle of a man's life how he
    encounters himself looking back
a hand on the bark of a poplar eyes still wondering at everything the
    flash of a wing the strike

you know how it works how you have to stand still letting the light
    climb up your trunk
you have to forget most things human this is not a place where
    anything has happened
you are a man you don't know how else to say it you are a man who
    has always sought god

there is a kind of indifference here hushed and slow it doesn't
    matter what you've been
it doesn't matter what you know you are almost a child here neither
    lost nor found not making strange
there is nothing you owe but the words you come to and those
    words are your seal

there is room for a mind between the high prairie sky and this
    scrappy undergrowth

how the air stirs shifting from one silence to another something
   about to happen
bare thickets in the fall a last pale rain arriving the way distant
   thunder hollows out the afternoon

the boy learns to stand among the trees a kind of listening at the
   edge of things
it's the step in that kills the man released into the open helpless and
   abandoned
if it wasn't for the rain who could live through the clearing if it
   wasn't for that mercy?

2

a slant of light that kind of silver light among the poplars that kind
   of sudden silence
you slow as you approach or it arrives a moment you might have
   dreamed or not
that kind of light stops your breath with fear you stand thin behind
   the last tree
staring at an emptiness filled with spear grass thistles and the end
   of world
so much missing there almost everything you know in the darkness
   of your memory

there is nothing so empty so quiet and becalmed in heat and
   doldrums and shivering at the edge
like the fox or deer you don't enter the field you gaze through the
   leaves and circle
you can't throw your life away you can't enter the abandon you long
   for can you?
a snake slides from a stone pile the hawk's shadow passing and
   clouds wavering in grass
you stalk the lit heart of earth slipping through scrub brush beneath
   the shimmer of leaves

is this disorder this stillness this clearing that shines like an eye this
   ring of bones?
you are a child always you are a child here baffled and waiting for
   the wind
you freeze as if you've been seen you don't breathe all you hear is
   the pulse in your ear
no it is something colder than childhood something unremembered
   and relentless

home ground where you learn to speak in two voices where you are
never at home

staring clarity the heart diminished to a fist how wind sweeps down
from a far cold place
there is nothing for this emptiness this moment where nothing is
and your eyes want to close from seeing
you can still smell the grease of birth on your arms your legs the
grease of your first birth
and you smell death that old smell of empty places quick as air
across your face
but you stand looking a faithless man standing his ground at the
edge of the clearing

3

when god tears at your heart or you think that's it you want that to
  be it angels perhaps or demons
when you need something to shape suffering something to hold it
  with intention

when the night deepens and you stand slow and waiting for your
  eyes to take in the trees
when you make your way through deadfall scraping your arms on
  the knuckles of a poplar

when the clearing flares with light the moon's brilliance carefully
  milking the thistle
when the stone pile glistens and cools sun's heat rising into the
  lowering sky

when nothing my god happens nothing in the vastness of your small
  rash living
when you have to laugh at the end of yourself at the god you think
  you've reached

when you crouch at a cold bethlehem as a constellation wheels
  across the clearing
when the offering you brought lies scattered at your feet and the
  only gift a broken heart

when you watch as you always have from the edge suddenly aware
  something breathes behind you
when you fear the darkness of bush the animal there but no safety
  in the clearing

when you find the body of the child struck down in its ecstasy of
   light and lamentation
when you step into the barefoot prayer at last when you pass into
   the open night

4

this is a precise place on your grandfather's farm a hard place by
    that you mean you stumbled on it
and it is hard with stones the brown grass spare and sharp its breath
    is harsh
this place holds nothing else a taut empty womb which birth has
    long abandoned

you surround the clearing with your stealth something more than
    animal something stray
gazing across you see where you were and will be again as you move
    around the world
there is nothing to lose anymore but you don't believe that as your
    eyes search for what is lost

grandfather knew this place it's where he dragged the bones of his
    dead animals
you hear his gruff voice the coarse words that urged the horses in
    their ringing harness
it's a language that wastes neither time nor tenderness but holds
    what a gaunt man knows of love

yes the horses grazed here their brown hides twitching with flies
    and the full smell of their lives
you watched them all afternoon slowly cropping their way to the
    heart of the clearing
standing there coppery in the sun long heads raised to the wind
    listening to you move

and you wonder who hauled their carcasses here later what voice
    called out that afternoon

the farm sinking like a ship into the memory of an old man toothless
    before his god
just the language is left what you learned about words meant
    beneath meaning

and how he strode into the clearing reins in hand turning his horses
    to release the load
how he disappeared again into the trees all lean and bone and
    calloused hands
how his voice faded the air closing behind him and you swung back
    into the silence

5

bones in the clearing and leaves turning in july this is the still month
    without rain
this is when you can hear the dog in the distance and you know he's
    coming for you
you are a boy and your smell hardly brushes the grass but the dog
    remembers

within your grandfather's rooted smell his hands on stone his sweat
    on a fence
his bleak years the way everything disappeared the way everything
    happened again
within the smell of one man's grasp reins handles and latches a
    woman's hair

within grandmother's death the smell of a thousand deaths the smell
    of snow on air
november bearing down grey as iron bands of breath from horses
    among bare trees
within the smell of the house blowing from an open door windows
    black with night

within the smell of your father's life his torn clothes and pride the
    smell of fresh-sawn planks
bending over his shirt with needle and thread and clearing his throat
    with a quiet cough
within the smell of *sen sens* the voice of a man in song his good eye
    on the notes

your small smell and the dog on your trail this is the place where
    you listen

this is the place to be alone where entrails vanish beneath the
  crow's clear eye
your smell is faint but the dog knows it and here leaning against the
  birch you know it too

6

this is not nature this scrub and thistle this clearing this is human
    this is broken land
this is war the brain this is the brilliant mind in love with horizons
    and desolation
the bones of barney and prince a rusting harrow in the weeds the
    ghost of a farmer at the plough
you hold brown photographs and a testament standing there among
    the columbine

all the things of god how they seduce you god within the thing you
    touch with your tongue
and you have to kill temptation don't you turn your back to it the
    world inside god
but it's hard killing god barefoot in the grass the long limbs of him
    the reach of him
and you can't the smell of him everywhere his spoor you track it in
    the night

something tore open this clearing some axe some plough but
    something more
before the shelterbelt before the dawson trail before the trails
    beneath the trail
first the hand fingerbones palm and heel then everything else the
    brain's cul de sac
dream broke open and bled the long line of the dream from ravines
    and foot broke a path

a killdeer's shrill cry calling rain its thin brown wings angling into
    flight this you know

the storm you weathered was nothing a little thunder lightning and
   it passed
always you've stood here watching and wanting to enter but waiting
   for a call
you've learned to answer no it's how you've managed to live love and
   refusal

it's something you know patience what you are like that bloody bird
   bowing the cattail
but the moment comes when you leave nothing left but the swaying
   reed
the moment arrives when you concede pride of thought the
   arrogance of belief
you want god you mean mother and father you think you hold love
   in your steadfast arms

lies you don't know what you want what it means all you know is
   your crouching
your hand reaching supplicant and you're squinting blue-eyed
   against the only light
you are an idiot your mouth gaping your arms aching with work you
   are almost invisible
the clearing is a suicide the mirror you want to smash and a mirage
   to dive into

you can't name god trying to live outside of that the cheap
   mechanics of civilization
this place is not nature the hand has touched it but the hand has
   done worse elsewhere
the idea the pattern sheer greed puts an end to things the process
   of eye mind and act
and you can't name that either your house leaning around its rotting
   timbers

so you return to the clearing the silent dog off its leash and it's a
quick step into family
you've heard the tales of voyage and grief you've read the journals
the details of gardens
you stand back to see you stand back for the necessary breath you
stand back for what can't be named
you've always worshipped in your anger in your distances in your
utter ignorance

7

a black-eyed susan blazes suddenly among the stones and brown
    stalks of grass
there is no veil here there are only your eyes there is only siloam
    and then the night

this is where you love where you drink yourself away this is a
    roadhouse to the end
your laughter is god's delight and when you come with your love
    there are earthy words

always you are returning you are human and you long for the place
    from which you came
on the way you empty your pockets but you no longer shake stones
    from your shoe

standing in the clearing you turn between where you were and
    where you were
and you know this is where you've always been the scent of your
    lover on the wind

your face among the leaves is someone else's the horse's large brown
    eye watching
you lie down in grass as seed and flower fall you lie down where
    your father lay

8

this is where your fathers brought death in their lives this is the
    place it was gathered
you squat here caught in the silence of sunday and your inside talk
    the sun at three o'clock

this is where you think you've arrived this memory or absence that
    has you hooked
face it nothing's there it's all done voices gone though they've woven
    their way into yours

the trees are gone too and the creek everything bulldozed into fields
    and amnesia
the edges have disappeared you can't enter or leave there is
    nowhere to pass through

the hum of flies at the cowshit a cry from a distant house you rise to
    your own height
the weight of your body slides through your shoes and once again
    you do not choose

you say no and mean yes one blanched skull where the clearing
    might have been
you nudge it with your foot a dog's life and that's enough your scent
    growing faint

9

you dress for winter because leaves have fallen and you can't hide
    your nakedness in the world
the sun glazes off snow's crust and the poplars' white bark
    richocheting through scraggy bush
sky glitters among the trees and then snow light and more light and
    your eyes blue with sky
you are barely there though the world is filled with the sound of
    your breathing
you move through your moment of heat breaking snow's skin step
    after slow step
there's nothing human anywhere only the quick whisky jack only
    that kind of thought
nothing buried nothing hidden nothing to recall only the slate of
    snow around you
yet there are your footprints what to make of them they always
    come from somewhere
though one day you'll turn and see nothing the trackless world that
    you know is there
and the whisky jack darts among the trees and disappears in the
    dark behind your eyes

26

10

your hands gummy with milkweed burrs on your pantleg you skirt
the clearing
a wind carrying ash the faint call of some animal but you no longer
turn to look

rain sways across the clearing you watch it arrive hear it rustling
among the leaves
you stand in your torn shirt drenched through and rain running
down your face

one more arrow at god then you unstring your bow there's really
nothing to strike
and something else the horses are released from their harness and
the dog where is the dog?

11

the dry smell of hay in a yellow afternoon blowflies busy around a
  small brown death
you know the orphan was here standing in disarray you know he
  waited for the lord
aspen leaves flickered in the light almost nothing moved it was a day
  no one arrived
that memory's gone and in the stubble a sparrow calls caught
  beneath the crow's spread wings
you know there's nothing to make of this the child grew away
  everything disappears to god

12

you come to him as a man in the heat of july the dog scratching
  bloated ticks with a hind leg
you sit on the bench someone has built in the clearing and you gaze
  at what you've known
you know there is something much wilder than you are you know it
  can't be named

what is it but finality what you're left with instead of an answer
  instead of solace
or not that at all but the answer you didn't expect or the question
  you couldn't shake
no it's the conversation you've always had inside the mull and grind
  of fear and love

none of that's right and who are you talking to this longing is such
  an unrelenting song
you are a stranger to him he gave you flesh and blessed you and
  that is enough
listen some men stand in their own smell wherever they are they
  can't walk away

13

almost hidden beside an aspen a deer's head eyes gazing across the
    clearing at you
that kind of momentary heed back and forth and a movement at the
    corner of your eye
you shift in time to see someone disappearing into the trees at least
    you think so
you watch the torn sky closing nothing else has changed though
    everything has moved
the face is gone now beside the aspen a red columbine and its dusty
    leaves

and you know it was jesus though you don't know why something
    about the stride
out of where you've come from voices across long rooms and fear
    out of what you've left
saviour and christ those terrible names those abject surrenders and
    hesitations
and back rooms where you fell on unwilling knees driven there by
    the weight of calvary
but always jesus turned from your humiliation you heard the door
    close behind him

smoke beneath the closed door the heat of hallways you could have
    lost your self in
your knees raw with love your eyes wide with disbelief you knew
    the end of world
and you knew nothing nothing you were trouble the stone in your
    father's shoe
heilger geist calling that tongue those voices the insinuations sung
    into your childish ear

october rain that version of eternity all night the drizzle that version
    of a little while

and it's all electricity though rain always stills you the storm of your
    birth day
yes what happens when the child is born wrong what to say about
    god's eye your eye
and you hear what you know rain and leaf the jerusalem tree the
    leaves of your dark book
balm of gilead ephraim nazareth rain falling through your menno life
    bruges the dnieper steinbach
everything so small detail detail the deaths maria klaas the dog
    bearded grass and thistle

14

so you've grown old and still here in this poverty of land and soft
  wind on your face
you have love this you know and you pray thanks you are not too
  old for her arms
you like to watch her when she's unaware of you and you are not in
  this world
she walks where she wants where you have been asleep or watched
  from the leaves
her eyes are dark returned from sorrow dark and hungry and you
  can't help yourself
you watch her in the clearing moving through your terrain and she
  turns to watch you
that's when you know that she draws you back her hand waking you
  and you are flesh
and only someone with her solitude could manage this could touch
  you alive

15

rain comes down that sparse night rain in october you feel the sad
  rhythm of fall
not sad not quite a whispering among the leaves as if something
  might be alive

your mother playing *träumerei* on the piano and singing you into
  dream with *wiegenlied*
you remember that desire to sing to meet the need in her voice to
  find the words

it's a trap of course there's not a damned thing you can do but reach
  for the notes
what you want is to sing anonymously you want to sing as if you are
  the voice of the world

now you listen to *peace piece* thinking it's rain on the leaves rain
  inside your head
thinking there's not a false note there's no presence outside the
  playing and no player

you imagine his hands hovering over the keyboard anticipation what
  is held back
and what is released his fingers thinking to the bottom of the key
  what can't be sustained

yes it's rain on poplar leaves on a wooden bench rain on a shed's tin
  roof those variations
it's a falling of rain and you're inside it and no it's not his song it's
  never his song

and this touches on what matters doesn't it not how you think about
the clearing but how you enter
this is about how you live here your mind moving without thought in
this home

16

a cold morning with hoar frost on branches quiet with snow and
　　breathless
the iron chime of harness and the muffled steps of horses among
　　boney trees
you are a boy warming your hands with a tin mug of tea a small fire
　　sinking in the snow
you are imagining what you will be you are imagining your lover you
　　are imagining your work
you can write your story in this clearing there is so much bareness
　　before your eyes
nothing written here no dark book no signs to read no ancient
　　meanings to weigh
tribes are forgotten clans and desert the sea and scars and flight the
　　anxiety of christ
there is no fear there are no second thoughts you feel snow melting
　　inside your boots
small tracks around grain stubble mice and buntings chickadees like
　　a child's scrawl
so that's written what's left what isn't asleep what's light and quick
　　and gone
you do not glimpse the day you will return on your knees you do not
　　know what you will need to live
the first exile begins here and the second you will gaze back often
　　from your distance
you burn your mouth with the tea you wake again already it's an old
　　ritual
you hear a snort but there are no horses in the world everything is
　　clear everything unseen

17

crisp air cuts into your lungs long shadows of aspen on lit snow not
    much is this still
not much speaks as well about you and you feel home in this thin
    wintry night
the owl watches and the hour shifts into the next you pause like
    breath on air

you love winter light at night the clearing cold and starry and far
    from earth
no need to raise your hand against the sun and your eyes widen to
    take everything in
you find nothing in too much light nothing but obscurity nothing but
    the thought of god

you pick your way through deadfall plunging sometimes to your
    knees listening to your breath
when you stop and stand you hear the blood flowing through your
    body's terrain
how can you be so sunken into earth and hardly on it at all or is it
    world you hardly know?

you don't see the wind rise but you hear it soughing through black
    spruce near the frozen slough
it's an old sigh that moves through you with everything you've
    known and what you can't
it is the groan of leaving of moving among bare trees toward what's
    open what's there

when you enter the clearing you are caught a stark animal tracked
    in the snow

you see only the dark circumference of the unbroken circle you've
  come from
you are wild in the bright snare laughing in this ambush this calm
  and fatal release

18

where is the lord without his cross dragging through the grass
where is the predator you dream?
what has passed through the clearing passes through you what
passes leaves its scars

there is no pride left in what you are time has not moved toward
you it slips by
your flesh is busy falling apart so that another will circle your bones
with these thoughts

you begin to know the lord's step that familiar sound behind he
wants nothing of you
he follows you for the day you want something of him there is
nothing necessary here

you could be wrong sound can fool you among the aspen and there's
light everywhere
this is a place you can say anything and anything is false this is a
place you can't go wrong

always the surprised deer leaps from the thicket it has trusted for
its sleep
the hawk on the fencepost turns its head to accommodate you with
its wild eye

19

nothing is saved and love lives only today in the hunger of your
   eager eyes
the child who carries you for a while the lover you've finally found
   to hold these days with you
for god men willingly murder men it has been so for long a crease
perhaps in the circle of the brain
for god men would hasten the world to their paradise for god men
   build their babel
some days you smell exhaust drifting through the trees it settles on
   the columbine
you hear the town siren at supper the workers walking home and
   the machine runs on
the town believes so hard they worship themselves thin and hardly
   anyone reaches for the wine
you fall asleep at the edge of the clearing when you wake snow has
   fallen for a million years
you have grown young and ancient you rise in the still air your
   breath in clouds before you
the shadow of a man beneath the moon struggling through the snow
   and night

20

you can stand where you are that's something stand and know
  where you are
snow drifts thick and soft you lose the world there's nothing to see
  and you gain your soul
can you speak that way can you speak as if it matters as if it really
  comes down to that?
you're exhausted by the dance of anything goes by the dance of
  nothing is known
and you're tired of the certainty of prophets of words that haven't
  passed through the heart
snow slants across the world wind picking up moaning through the
  spruce and pine
sometimes you wish you weren't human but it's love that stops you
  and throws you down
your lover asleep near you her wrist glistening with bracelets breath
  slipping through her lips
there's nothing you can make of this it won't fit in the book it can
  only change the world
god with his anger christ with his miracles you wanted to believe it
  all but it hasn't worked well
and yet you saw your father go with jesus in his eye you have to
  believe this was so
a man at the end left with nothing but his lord the ground of his
  dignity and his glory
you can't take that from him for a moment you have to believe as he
  believed
but it's the absence of this man you enter a wistfulness you can't
  explain you call it love
snow hooks in the branches of the aspen and you think you'd go
  anywhere with the lord

your heart so full your eyes cold as stone your children somewhere
on this earth

21

the scree of a red-winged blackbird the only sound in a light breeze
  spinning aspen leaves
you slouch half-asleep on the bench a northern man dreaming his
  eastern love
wide awake behind drooping eyelids wondering your way across
  wide distances
jerusalem shanghai and victoria the old ones carried her through
  desert harbour and sea
your hands remember her face remember her wrist your hands
  know the east
she walks from her father's household slender and black-haired she
  crosses the street
sometimes she leans on the balcony's rail watching late afternoon's
  light in the beech trees
she turns to you as a familiar stranger one meant from long ago one
  met in the doorway
you love the honey of her mouth you didn't know you would enter
  the testaments like this
she moves quietly through her life she knows the shadow at the end
  of days
evening arrives in the trees birds go still you straighten on the
  bench and shiver
night is filled with speech an old sibilance voices from all the graves
  of the world
you have always listened tried hopelessly to understand and have
  sometimes understood
but what's understood disappears you swallow what's on the tip of
  your tongue
don't question the pleasure of her body and her words don't
  question the moment of love

you stand at the close of day alone among the trees you inhale and
smell her scent

wind subsides and grows cold with stars the prairie sky so clear the
earth so dark

you look at her in the late light you look at her for long minutes look
at her lying naked
her eyes watch only your eyes as they slowly caress her caressing
the length of her
you delay your hands they want to see her too your hands have
known her well
you gaze across the clearing this place the hawk surveys this place
where it will die
you know each time that you have hardly seen her each time you
look a last time
this is ravage this looking this is the demand of the raptor's gaze a
measuring
and this is the tenderness of civilized man this is the love that has
been learned slowly

so much moves through you lineage man and animal and you are
almost still
you stoop over her with a desire that can't be said you long beyond
what can be done
you look at her because you know that when you follow your hands
there will be a close
so you lean further and stare your eyes narrowing toward that
inevitable threshold
for a moment your eyes meet and you are shaken by her desire by
her deep call
she wants your rapacious eye she wants that instant between the
gaze and the motion
and then you know she wants to see your eyes close always she
wants to see your eyes close

you look at her in the late light her eyes following yours as they
   slowly rake her
she does not see what you see she finds only your eyes seeing and
   this is all she is given
and you do not know what she knows of you your crouch there
   suddenly bare
this is when you need stone or something rooted as you loosen into
   embrace
there is nothing possible in the clearing god passes through and you
   are left looking
she reaches for you her hand at your face her bracelets shimmering
   for a moment
you're awake in this light a hawk's wing caught by sun as it tilts
   abruptly toward earth

23

a distant hammer from a farm or perhaps from town a slow hammer
near dusk
a bird in the silence after the hammer a yellowhead's rasp from the
marsh then nothing
light sliding down the trees suddenly a moment that has nothing to
do with day or night
you feel the absence it must have always been this way a hesitation
the earth impalpable

born of no one where are they all the long line of lives born of each
other of want
as usual everything is true it can't be spoken not well not as light
vanishes and faith begins
but you were never a man of faith you follow your eyes your ears
you follow the scent
and sometimes you stand in your tracks chagrined that you've run
into your self

air stirs for a moment it could be one of those nights when
something is set loose
the way wind muscles through clumps of scrawny jack pine with a
low roll
how the earth grows huge around you old old voices of wind and
then driving rain
anything could happen but nothing does the air grows still and
you're waiting

it could be longing it tips so easily from waiting that human flaw
memory looking ahead

you want something to hold something to plant among the pine
among the aspen
sometimes where you come from means so little those hands and
tongues those words
you're always waiting as if it begins with you no as if it began a day
and a night before

train wheels rumble a long way off you remember someone in a
hurry to meet them
you turn a found knife over in your hand wipe it clean on your pants
and test its edge
flashes along the horizon thunder nearly a hundred miles west and
crawling south
the world is with you and you of the world a hammer ringing alone
in the town

24

willow and balsam apparitions a shiver in tall grass always
     something has passed
what you see in the corner of your eye slipping by and out of sight
     this enters your heart
so much remains from where you've been sparks from the track
     stray notes on the piano
you don't yet have heaven's eye that day will come today you love
     what you see

you stand inside the smell of approaching thunder the abeyance in
     that darkening
leaves tremble a moment before the wind arrives before it sets the
     trees thrashing
and rain blinds you stifles all sound except its own relentless
     drumming on shed and ground
and then it ceases suddenly dripping and everything emerges to
     inhale a new earth

the clearing changes with swift clouds and light the breath of a
     breeze and a cooper's hawk
a marsh wren struck in flight and carried broken to a bough feathers
     drifting to earth
shreds of the dead body seeded everything silent a sparrow fleeing
     deeper into the bush
sometimes the bench is empty and no one listens for anything no
     one watches the world

25

you watch the red-tail on the fence post it's there every day
    watching for movement
you love when it skims low some elusive prey darting underground
    in the stubble

you're thinking of the world you came from the kind of wisdom that
    bound you
work and belief jesus and christ you're remembering the back steps
    of the church
old stories run through your head voices that wanted the best
    wanted your surrender
they wanted you to see your father in his coffin a gaunt face a
    carpenter's folded hands
and you what did you want to see what lay in death what lay behind
    that beloved body?

what you knew was that the town would bury you and love would
    throw the first handful
jesus walked through your life every day but they called him christ
    always something to bang into
and you pedalling your bicycle out of town finding the clearing with
    its silence and its heat
creeping through the underbrush to watch your grandfather
    working the fields
his far-off voice another voice in your life and you learning how to
    listen to them all

there are matters you want to dispute and others you want to praise
    it doesn't matter

or it matters but only to get you through to dusk and uncertainty to
    3 a.m. and something more
you can't help but laugh your holy hours sift to ash drift away to
    settle in the grass
you had grace and were fatherless always leaving home always
    leaving what you held
so much has been chiselled in stone you want to brush the dust
    from his shoulders comb it from his hair

you know how much you still want and you catch your breath filled
    with longing
a longing for the weight of things a book in your hand a hand the
    human body
you stand aside so you can hear so you can see the columbine and
    black eyed susan
the wheels of a wagon have crushed long grass your grandfather you
    think but he's dead
and it's not his clearing and it's not yours yet this is where you have
    come to claim your ghosts

late afternoon arrives cold to your bones you throw on your coat
    this is where you find your flesh
and you stand alone next thing to heaven and nothing there but
    hawk and mind

26

barefoot jesus coughing in the rain in samaria no one good in sight
    and the figs not ripe
you imagine a fever and you imagine his thought sometimes you
    almost know what he saw

a man stumbles to the water to wash his blind eyes and opens them
    to an old world
does he hear a sparrow darting through air or does he enter
    darkness once again?

you love the story of assisi preaching to the birds calling on them to
    sing praises to the lord
and they sang their wings fluttering the songbirds sang but you
    wonder where the hawk flew

you lose the world over and over love is unruly the disorder that
    brings good it can it can
it's what you hold here your children your lover death in your heart
    it's possible

who is it you hear speak as you speak sing as you sing what voices
    live in you?
a harsh call in the clearing and that breath that deep breath you
    take from the lord

träumerei

poem for mother's birthday

march's daughter born on the soft side of winter but short of
blossoms and the river's flow
as if I was there I saw her all spirit in a dress a shape before my
world began
a skinny girl on stilts or a heron stepping through shallows her eyes
bright for living

in the winter she searched for gifts in the wind-scooped hollow
around the oak a fox lurking near the coop
when spring came she watched lightning once it sizzled in a ball
through the screen
and it lit her up the words inside the song on her tongue her wonder
on fire

and then I forgot her the child gone to labor and belief the girl
become wife
a mother pulling a sleigh toward the post office a blue wintry sky
and the crunch of her feet
I remember that sound echoing in the world and I remember a voice
clear as glass

at night with wolves in the snow and precise stars through a million
miles of thin air
her voice in the kitchen singing *the ballad of sir patrick spens* his
men long sunk to the bottom
and nothing but sea and wind and his floating hat and it's so still but
for the stars and her soprano

later her work done she sits at the piano the whisper of pages
turning and I know what's next

her fingers on the keys as she pauses for a long moment and I wait
   and I wait for those first notes
träumerei drifting down the hall through the crack at the door kept
   open so I can see light

I'm human a human child as I slide toward sleep and dream and all
   the icons of memory
long before the crucifixion that broken sky and weeping long before
   the upper room
to the mother and child crossing a ravine hand in hand toward what
   they do not know

becoming human with love and god all that confusion mother and
   child lost on some forgotten trail
sinking a stone down a well a lady at the well the soft hem at her
   slender feet
and memory is so watery and born wild from your eyes all that's
   been outside the story

there are moments when I know the trail how it winds in and out of
   a dreamy night
always remembering her shoe in snow and schumann clear as stars
   down the hall
the first mother and mine on her birthday the astonishment of love
   so fierce

I see her on a swing her legs pumping for height grandchildren
   scrambling around her
and she's always singing about ancient days the shannon the volga
   or the cold north sea
and sometimes I think she's a sailor with that mischief in her eyes
   and the song that won't run out

light in june

the yukon flows green through whitehorse swans flying low into the
    faded yellow light behind the mountains
at night the sky hangs cobalt blue as if the sun never left but lies out
    of sight waiting for dawn
nothing sleeps not fully everything pausing for a moment like the
    sun within the trees and the river

always light being born the prairie moon shining on a white shirt
    forgotten on the line
moonlight sifting among shadows in the garden corn stalks shivering
    and lilac leaves soaked in silver
shapes near the church move silently outside the streetlight's arc
    nothing's human without details

light at an angle or false light at night reflected through a white
    curtain shimmering in the window
everything is possible at night something born out of that place of
    drowning where the child stares through walls of water
swimming toward light a baptism and an endless dying until dying
    the child comes alive a falling light

like light from nowhere we are born and like light we step toward
    nowhere alive and aflame
light bursting from seedlings the field's dark soil lit one morning in
    pale green fire who would have thought
where there was nothing there is light and light is nothing you can
    hold the flash off a spoon turning in a cup

living beneath the northern borealis or the dusky rose aura of a
    distant fire the sun ashen through smoke

a prairie storm boiling grey and blue torn by lightning and the
volcanic cauldron of the hidden sun
it's too much there's too much world and the world nothing but light
behind shadows

we see almost none of the light in our lives our hands raised before
us fingers splayed against the sun
our eyes squint to keep light out or we'd die from fire we'd perish
blind in the blaze of world
but like magdalen there are moments for each when we stand
astonished and witness to light

october poem

lost in itself a cat stretches on the porch no quickness left it gazes
    across the strewn lawn turns slumping back to sleep
the air is thick with golden light droning bees slow and drunk lifting
    heavily from apples oozing on the ground
everything's drying with fullness the second hand crawling around
    the clock a ball game drifting through the radio
a barefoot girl in the garden sprawls among roots and withered
    rhubarb weaving a rope of reeds

it's a satiated month people wander through cemeteries reading
    stones and entering old stories
we begin to leave the place we've lived and move into time going
    blind as moles in the dark
the last things of summer still before us but utterly changed a
    breeze suddenly filled with shivers
a boy hangs onto the silence of the willow his memories shifting to
    dream as his eyes look in

we've gathered the riches of earth in our aprons and baskets we
    have filled our cellars against the long winter
we pause like everyone before us has ever paused the hunch of
    death in our bones
this has happened forever this moment when we know what we are
    and where we've come from
october flows in our veins besotted we look back thankful and
    hesitant in our remembering

imagining mother and child who left their footprints long before
    history glancing at the sky

the chance and choice of seasons and weather the way almost
    nothing happens as intended
the ambiguity of our spirit clear or possessed a slender arm in a
    dance or the brain's brutality
we work through the year blackberries and bramble through the
    hours toward evening

for a moment there is no need in our bodies though something
    haunts us as night absorbs day
walking beneath streetlights in the clatter of acorns on a shed's tin
    roof we reach out to hold hands
this isn't romance or chivalry we reach out of loneliness bare trees
    creaking with the age
we are this species in debt to the earth facing the hunger and cold
    with our companions

november poem

november's ankle-deep in snow working its way along the railroad
    toward a midnight sun
november fills with flurries so soft they tickle the back of your bare
    hand and catch on your lashes
early november is the pause between seasons between centuries
    when we look back with hope forward in fear
how do we approach the end of things now this century how do we
    say farewell in a blizzard?

the century began with bayonets and dancers nijinsky descending
    heavily to the killing floor no longer embraced by air
the snow and blood of a century moving so swiftly beneath its
    burden the weight of machine and thought
he looked for another kind of grace heavy boots and treading a
    desperate game of fox and goose
nijinsky dancing in the asylum his own and the world's the last home
    of lost memory

november is a russian month with its thistle bass and soprano the
    deep solace of voices surrendering to a sundered time
ancient peasants in their knowing ignorance all scythe and time
    gobbing on their floors and crossing themselves
the spent casings of shells like seeds beneath first snow winter
    wheat and a promise of hunger
and they sing of sorrow and bandits and wandering the liturgy of the
    outcast and the lover of eternity

the century turns in november with its turmoil and an eye on
    january cold and hard and new

nijinsky dreamed this death giving way to gravity and trying one last
time to shape it human
but human is a trickster's shape clever and greedy for bullets greedy
for paradise
the dancer falls in the snow frozen feet in rags and eyes on the sun
that won't go down

flurries fly in november across the world a russian choir sings of
easter and christmas just ahead
those voices hold much but we hardly hear them the world's radio
so very loud
the railroad's buried the crosses of war leaning into the wind the
wars forgotten in monuments
and the machines the machines rumble on the highways we think
they're ready for the blizzard

december poem

jello's hardening on the porch christmas punch cooling in a drift the
   shadow of a fox steps lightly behind a hedge
who's that singing *hark the herald angels sing* off key in the pale
   light falling from the kitchen window?
it's the barber with a comb in his back pocket the town fool and
   henry with his hohner harmonica
they've forgotten words and no song book but it doesn't matter they
   haven't all forgotten the same ones

henry's hammering at the door the harmonica frozen to his lips and
   he stumbles in to thaw it off
the barber with his bowl haircut reaches for walnuts and cracks
   them between his splintered teeth
there's talk of blizzards and 1934 or was it 43 the war rations the
   good old days
and henry with blood on his teeth wonders if he can have another
   mandarin orange

I'm remembering the fox caught her in the corner of my eye and I
   go out to find her
there is no distance like december's distance how far across the field
   how far to the star of the east
the clarity of air takes my breath the fool's shadow stretching from
   the window across the white lawn
there's no fox can't find her prints a ghost of christmas past and I
   unplug the car for a drive

skidding down #12 past akron where father was born past kokomo
   road toward la broquerie to find a drink

snow banked on the shoulders keeps me honest the radio cranked
  high on *born on the bayou*
drifting snow across the windshield erases everything but the
  moment and that's filled with past
winter dreams of sleep hands numb and forgotten the face a mask
  for the dangerous spirit inside

how do you live with snow van gogh's stars roiling in a dark blue sky
  a perfect stillness only cold can bring?
long nights with the moon dazzling in sheets off the fields the howl
  of a far-off dog or coyote
how do you live with snow sane and clear with the nudge of love in
  your heart and the fox long gone?
old henry's dead nothing left but shreds of skin on his harmonica
  and the memory of a song

signature

the movement of his hand across paper was not an embellishment
   but the rehearsal of his name
what he wanted to shape was a motion something of the spirit that
   gave decency its depth

a man practices his signature filling scrap paper with his name over
   and over again
a man enters his signature he repeats the rhythm of his hand and
   the sounding of his name

his name written all over the sheet torn from a scribbler like the
   devotions of a pilgrim
what a man has outside of love is the work he has woven to his
   name the honour of his hand

he sat there at the kitchen table with the wealth of his name and the
   certainty of his god
a man belongs on earth with his children a man works his way
   through his name

kaddish for the old man

your dark eyes and fedora your straight muscled back and your long
stride
these are gone though I remember everything though I forget
everything forever amen
it is a poor son who does not hold his father who does not carry him
toward the next death
I do that it can't be helped but I may not be the vessel you hoped to
leave behind

I stand on my balcony the beech trees are bare and I don't know
where you are
perhaps in that grave where we laid you but I am child enough to
think the sky
what I know will leave with me that evening I saw how empty your
last room became
I took in the emptiness and circled it the one thing you knew about
me my relentlessness

I start with you standing still in the garden I start with me staring
from the raspberry canes
I wonder who you are or where because I can see you're not there
you're lost and I have no father
you're caught between entrances though always one seems an exit
the other a closed door
there are many moments like this you standing knee-deep in west
hawk lake or us in the basement before the furnace

but you are my father calling me into the world the world you are so
afraid of

is this where something goes awry your uncertain call and the boy
   stubborn at the garden's edge
you wake from your reverie and turn toward the back window
   where your love sings
sleeves rolled above your elbows the late sun flashing off your
   glasses how you wanted heaven

and now I'm as old as you ever were or will be as old as I need to be
   to stand for you
I have made my life out of you I am something you didn't know blue
   eyes in the mirror
there's no lightning on the horizon old man no thunder it's a quiet
   rain arriving
earth remembers us for a moment but the garden has gone wild and
   the stone rolls away

nothing but the weather

time passes slowly tonight I hear it in the cold rain drizzling on the
    street in the radio rounding to the top of the hour again and
    again
tonight the rain doesn't still me my heart irregular and knocking at
    the door tonight is fear and I can hardly breathe
father's diary is filled with weather I read my way through the
    seasons a good man in his garden wanting nothing but the love
    he has
I wonder what's different between us I want the same though I don't
    have it that's not the difference it has something to do with the
    garden

beloved I have loved you all the way and still not found you I love
    you anyway to keep my soul
I have been wild in the garden it's worn me I've been thrown out
    nothing makes sense and I've accepted even that
my diary is a hunter's log all stealth and intensity as he tracks
    himself turning in turning in with his gun
I sleep without a body no sleepy voice drifting through my night in
    love there is a beginning and an end

god is desire in my heart my brain the desire to burn away the
    pages the house of words the church of belief
almost an empty man the plough furrowing through scars and scars
    you'd think something would grow
looking for a straight-backed lord the stance of spirit all bone and
    standing nothing wan or frail
looking for a clear prayer no sermon no pretty please no fine blind
    words of poem or song no weeping

small rooms

what matters happens in small rooms a call a letter what comes
    after the intention
the conversation within a man or woman the time taken to find the
    right words
where there is intimacy between thought and word the world grows
    a little still

what matters happens where there's not too much room and the
    walls lean in
the conversation that's possible when the windows freeze over with
    frost on the sill
where there's no one to hear you and change the words the world
    grows a little old

what matters happens where you sit with your elbows on the table
    your feet on the floor
the conversation that rattles through your head all night and leaves
    you worn in the morning
where there are no footprints in the snow and no face at the
    window the world grows forgotten

the man who licked stones

the man in the long coat licked stones memorizing the world's first
fire on his tongue

he didn't have time to speak though he had nothing else he hadn't
come to words

his slow hands hung from the stillness of his torn sleeves reaching
only to touch what he might remember

with his hands he carefully brushed dust from stones with his
tongue revealed their rose or cobalt blue

he walked outside town on gravel roads he walked outside love too
close to worship to say

around him earth's rubble and striations sign and witness of the
forge he longed to find

his mouth craving volcanoes the taste of ash and rain his mouth
ground stones in his sleep

I thought he would vanish one day spellbound in his cellar among
the coal and roots

I thought in the end he might walk into the river with his heavy
pockets but there was no such privilege for him

with the years I forgot him or he became a shape I couldn't see
wandering around town

I don't know if he took form again or if it was time for me to see but
I saw him emerge like a photograph in its bath

he was walking past the church he reeled suddenly with a stiff-
legged pivot and fell straight on his back

no one falls like that the body in surrender to gravity no one falls as
if nothing matters and nothing did

his eyes glistening like wet sapphires in snow his dead eyes looked
through us seeing their way into stone

older than love

these bones are older than love no lord god in my skin it's just this
    fever that comes with words this disease my darling of the mirror
no one plays our song anymore never did no regrets not longing for
    anything shaven and hopeless as a convict in an open field
there's nowhere to run when the borders disappear yesterday a
    hominid I died on a riverbank today you've found my bones
there's nothing to the 21st century everyone's all eyes slaves and
    worshippers and everyone's in movies

all the light in the world the way a ship moves through a still
    harbour an oak tree creaking in a wind it's been known
a cello hollows out a doorway a mother sings her child asleep old
    stories that are not old enough caught in their romance
my body growing old remembers a touch from somewhere deep
    down in the rift some moment a million years ago
trying to remember memory how it began and what came before
    that moment when I saw myself or wasn't it me at all?

there's nothing can be done about it love's here now hand in hand
    with god strange how we set them against each other
they both slipped in love during the heat of day and god cool as a
    midnight stiletto between my ribs
I'd give anything to see the old ones grandma and grandpa at the
    river burying a child and gazing at each other
perhaps love and fear for a moment the rainy season closing in and
    no photographs no prayers to disappear in

the crow's perched in the jerusalem tree he's been there forever is
    he looking for love has he seen god?

that hesitation in the rift rising on two legs called for the first time
by a nameless pain a desolation and nothing having changed
found wanting amongst the baboons and acacias thinking of home
and returning through volcanic ash to the fire
absence grows the question an emptiness something nagging a word
on your tongue and desire

no one at the door

dishevelled or an untidy room good god untidy living and love bereft
uncombed and combing the woods with bare hand and lamp
this is simple playing the grizzled word without a prayer
the doldrums and slack-sailed a sad-sacked scraping
if I don't collapse I'll collapse if you know what I mean
groaning between the long dry seasons a rain of heaven
an unbearable laziness unkempt and crazy for an easy out
tongue uprooted and stupid blabbering toward desolation
and no one at the window no one at the door

the candle that rooted me gone to earth though not the light
how it enters the cellar again and again to find fire
and always an ember is found and everything begins again
there is no other way to master death or to die than by this cinder
stubborn humans in heat with their hands and work and gawking
man and woman on the beach lit by the monstrous sun going down
but there are no dark clouds no wind and no thunder clap
someone graceful swimming to shore

but that was a dream that was the arrival of a guest
and the road is filled with such strangers and their silent steps
what drifts by passing for world the things I love and praise
drifting like rivers like rain in sheets across my wide-eyed staring
unrelenting a shapeless sky and this bony standing up shade
the way there's nothing there beyond the swinging door
endless heaven before me my shoes covered in dust
torn clothes hanging on a skeleton his hat on a rock
and he's praying at the useless sky he's lost in desire

there's a time for the hand raised against the hidden man

and a time to surrender at the foot of the stairs
ah my lovers and cousins I have been your enemy
I can no longer speak for myself I have spoken too much
wanting to be human again at home in the commotion of love
this agitation the gull circling around its broken wing
there is nowhere to go I have walked through many doors
retrieving my heart from a woman I loved
I once held a perfect foot in my hand

come what you are and who like the slapping of rain on stone
a serenity not death dear god not sleep but blindness
the voice of leaves stirred silver by a breeze
come from books and prayers come from wherever you are met
I can't think my way through it can't imagine what I know
the piano upstairs sounds like a moon in june
come blind as fathers in their unspoken grief
right there in bethesda his lovely hand in water
come turn my face toward you

give me flesh and give me wine

rain comes down on east third like manna at christmas like spirit
    vanish to flesh
the guttural body singing its memory as it corrodes toward memory
    a voice not here
thinking in things what is felt by hands even as it disappears or what
    is almost heard
a bird dreaming its music toward morning first light waking the song
    like a struck match
the flare of light in air a momentary stench of sulfur and the quick
    day gone cold
so a fox lopes across the moonlit snow a star fluttering in the
    firmament

it is so far to travel hand to mouth words and fingers the carpentry
    of desire
hammering smoke into framework something to hold us intact and
    understood
so far to travel in footprints this human disease of wondering what
    was there
how present absence can be you almost smell it sometimes absence
    isn't absence at all
but memory like the wind wears away at the world and though wind
    remains memory does not
so lovers walk beneath an arch almost as if they'd never lived before

there's nowhere to go in the desert but further in there's a time to
    live without doors
caught wide open the heart bleeding into sand and the bird's
    shadow drifting by

that's how it goes some nights your doubt and desire the most awful
   perfect belief
not much room to turn in your narrow bed lots of time to find the
   end of yourself
what you imagine goes nowhere such a long and difficult death
   looking for your feet
so the hawk scours earth with its ravenous gaze a consuming fire

the king calls for meat and drink and jesus is born and in
   remembering something dies
child can speak and will crouched in the doorway moving from
   womb to shambles
and the innocence of stone and water the marvel of the wide-eyed
   human brood
the king calls for meat and drink a communion the body dancing
   drunk and ghostly
there's so much deep pleasure in the world it makes spirit of us and
   cadavers
so a hand rests on a windowsill and rain falls against the glass

first river

there is rain on the coast and snow on the plains we are on our own
   and next to godless
turning on a false pivot of time here on a fault line home and
   harbour where I sail away
my love walks along sidney spit dark-haired and stolen from the
   stories of her ancient family
where do you walk when the footprints have been blown away but
   solomon calls?

beneath a blue umbrella I turn from the future looking for the holy
   city and the river
somewhere snow slashes across a mile road there is that and the
   wolf and the human hand
the great machinery we worship is nothing but what we've made
   because we can
what we know is death and the divining stick what we know is the
   child barging through the door

in the backyard father tossed his first child into the air spinning
   around in rapture
I remember him with his camera lining us up at the edge of harvest
   and the pale sky
the air was white with chaff and nostalgia the thresher's long black
   belt snaking through the day
I remember the stinging heat and shirtsleeves I remember the
   waterboy bringing the bucket down

leaning against grandfather's well I was drinking clear water cold as
   a bell on my tongue

remember the girl in a stream holding her skirts at her waist sinuous
sea weed on her leg?
ah that was at the beginning so long ago before the siberian shuffle
and the goosestep
stephen hero and the weight of a soul and dish water running down
the drain

mother hanging wash singing holy city you can almost see the bride
in veils of morning
and a long-eyed man in the garden the devastation of heaven a
lonely mind passing through
looking down the furrow a singletree and hand loading the stone
boat beneath a winter star
perhaps this is how we continue a man splashes cold water on his
face at dawn

what I love is the drift of day the way clouds accumulate the way we
are drawn to prayer
how my chair scrapes as I leave the supper table and my love turns
to glance at me
I love night with rain at the window I shiver at the voice calling the
child home
divining clear water the first river beneath the willow everything
turning on the sound of rain

Notes

träumerei, the title of the second section of the book, and referred to in several poems, is a piano piece which is part of Robert Schumann's *Kinderszenen*, Op. 15.

wiegenlied is a lullaby (also known as "Guten Abend, gut' Nacht") written by Johannes Brahms.

peace piece is a piano solo, written and performed by Bill Evans, on his album *Everybody Digs Bill Evans*.

give me flesh and give me wine is a line from "Good King Wenceslas."

hark the herald angels sing is a Christmas carol.

born on the bayou is a song written and sung by John Fogarty with Creedence Clearwater Revival.

the ballad of sir patrick spens is, of course, an old English ballad.

Acknowledgements

Some of these poems were previously published in: *CVII, Event, Malahat Review, New Quarterly, READ Society, Rhubarb*, the *New Delta Review*, and the anthologies *15 Canadian Poets x 3* (Oxford University Press, 2001), *Mocambo Nights: Poetry From the Mocambo Reading Series* (Ekstasis Editions, 2001), and *Following the Plough: Recovering the Rural* (Black Moss Press, 2000). Several poems were produced on CBC Radio (Manitoba) with producer Janet Dirks. Patrick Friesen is grateful to Beach Holme Publishing for permission to reprint "the man who licked stones" from *Carrying the Shadow* (Beach Holme Publishing, 1999).

Patrick Friesen's web site: www.patrickfriesen.com